# Champion for Children's Health

# Champion for Children's Health

*A Story about
Dr. S. Josephine Baker*

by Greg Ptacek
illustrations by Lydia M. Anderson

A Carolrhoda Creative Minds Book

Carolrhoda Books, Inc./Minneapolis

*To Jessica Maile Speetjens*

Library of Congress Cataloging-in-Publication Data

Ptacek, Greg.
    Champion for children's health : a story about Dr. S. Josephine Baker /
by Greg Ptacek; illustrated by Lydia M. Anderson.
        p.    cm. — (A Carolrhoda creative minds book)
    Includes bibliographical references.
    Summary: A biography of the doctor who, along with other achieve-
ments, was among the first to act on the idea that preventative medicine
and health care for children is a function of government.
    ISBN 0-87614-806-2
    1. Baker, S. Josephine (Sara Josephine), 1873-1945. 2. Health officers—
New York (N.Y.)—Biography—Juvenile literature. [1. Baker, S. Josephine
(Sara Josephine), 1873-1945. 2. Women Physicians. 3. Health officers.]
I. Anderson, Lydia, ill. II. Title. III. Series.
RA424.5.B33P76    1994
610'.92—dc20                                                93-10482
[B]                                                             CIP
                                                                 AC

Manufactured in the United States of America

1  2  3  4  5  6  –  P/MA  –  99  98  97  96  95  94

# Table of Contents

New England Paradise 7

Determined to Be a Doctor 14

Hell's Kitchen 24

The Fight for Children's Health 36

Right to Vote, Right to Health 48

Winning the Fight 57

Bibliography 63

# ① New England Paradise

Thinking about what a fine sight she would make at the party, six-year-old Sara Josephine Baker put on her lacy white dress with the blue sash, her light blue stockings, and her light blue leather shoes. While the rest of her family was still dressing, she sneaked outside to the front lawn of the family's elegant home. She perched herself on the horse block next to the road, and like a proud peacock, waited for the neighborhood to admire her in all her finery.

The only passerby, however, was a small black girl, about her age. Her dress was old and ragged. She was thin and hungry looking. The little girl stared at Josephine in her beautiful outfit.

Suddenly Josephine felt heartsick. She couldn't stand the idea that she had so much and the other girl had so little.

Josephine promptly took off all of her clothes—including her underwear—and gave everything to the stranger. The girl scampered away with joy. Then Josephine walked back into her house stark naked! Fortunately, her parents understood her kind gesture.

Born on November 15, 1873, in Poughkeepsie, New York, Josephine was the third child of Orlando Daniel Baker and his wife, Jenny Harwood Brown. Arvilla, Josephine's eldest sister, had died in infancy, and Mary, her other sister, was sickly. In contrast, Josephine was strong and adventuresome.

From the beginning, though, it was clear to Josephine that her father had wished for a son. "Trying to make it up to Father for being a girl," she remembered, "did turn me into a tomboy type in the early days. I was an enthusiastic baseball player and trout fisher." Her family called her "Jo."

A successful attorney, Orlando was one of the leading citizens of Poughkeepsie. During his career, he served as city attorney, as president of the board of education, and as a Democratic nominee for Congress. He was quiet and reserved by nature, but a loyal friend and warm, attentive father.

Orlando was also a devoted fisherman. He loved nothing better than to cast a line into Balsam Lake in the nearby Catskill Mountains or into one of the many lakes and streams in Dutchess County, New York. "By the time I could stand alone I was taught to cast a line," Jo remembered.

When she was three, a son was finally born—Robert. Jo grew especially close to Robbie, and the two of them would accompany their father on his fishing trips.

If Orlando was quiet and reserved by nature, Jo's mother, Jenny, was just the opposite—"gay, social and ambitious," as Jo recalled. Jenny came from a distinguished family of New England educators. One of her relatives had cofounded Harvard University.

Jenny had attended the respected Vassar College—one of the first women's colleges. It had been founded in Poughkeepsie in the late 1870s. Though she never graduated, Jenny remained interested and active in education after her marriage. She often hosted parties for the students and faculty of Vassar at the Baker home, which was nicknamed "The Vassar Annex." Consequently, young Josephine came to know many well-educated men and women, including the famous astronomer, Maria Mitchell.

Jo and Mary attended a private school, which was run by the Misses Thomas. An experimental school, it had no graded exams, marks, or report cards. The classes were informal, with only three or four girls in each group. The students were able to work at subjects at their own pace. Jo learned to set her own goals, and meet them.

At home, Jo was taught by her mother how to sew, bake bread, and put up jams. The Bakers lived in a big house staffed with servants, so the Baker children had no real chores. Jo was free to enjoy all of the activities open to a wealthy New England girl growing up in the nineteenth century: taffy pulls, formal luncheons, dances, clubs, afternoon teas, card parties, hayrides, clambakes, and picnics. As a special treat, the entire family would take a boat down the Hudson River to New York City to attend the theater.

Left to themselves, Jo and Robbie would row together on the Hudson River. In winter, there was ice-skating, bobsledding, and ice yachting. When the circus came to town, they would sneak away from home and spend the night watching the workers put up the Big Tent.

In the spring of 1890, sixteen-year-old Josephine was beginning to make plans to attend her mother's alma mater, Vassar. Jo was looking forward to attending college. But that changed in a matter of three months.

In early March, Robbie came down with a fever. The fever lingered a week and then began to rage. A noted physician was called, but within a few days, Robbie was dead. His illness had been diagnosed as "an inflammation of the bowels." Later they discovered he had died of a disease known as typhoid fever.

At the time, there were no such things as water-treatment plants. The residents of Poughkeepsie drew their water directly from the Hudson River. The river, however, was polluted with sewage from a hospital upstream that treated many patients with typhoid. Robbie was among the first victims of a typhoid epidemic that swept the city.

Robbie was fondly remembered in the local newspaper: "He was a very bright and intelligent lad for one of his years and was widely known and loved."

Orlando Baker was devastated by his son's death and never recovered from the trauma.

Within a few weeks, he, too, developed a raging typhoid fever and died.

Jo was heartbroken. She later wrote: "We were an understanding trio—my father, my brother, and myself—and when they died so close together it seemed [there was] very little left to live for."

Adding to the sorrow and strain, the family had no income and only modest savings. The household servants had to be dismissed, and Josephine had to abandon her plans to attend Vassar. "It was immediately evident," said Jo later, "that somebody would have to get ready to earn a living for all three of us—my mother, my sister, who had always been delicate and a semi-invalid, and myself. I considered myself elected."

# Determined to Be a Doctor

Soon after her father's funeral, Josephine announced to her mother and relatives that she wanted to become a doctor. This left "both sides of the family aghast," Jo remembered, "at the idea of my spending so much money in such an unconventional way. It was [an] unheard of, harebrained, and unwomanly scheme."

A female doctor was certainly a rarity in the late 1880s, and what was more, none of

Josephine's relatives had ever been in the medical profession. The idea had first occurred to Jo years back, when she was ten years old and had hurt her knee. The injury was so severe that she had had to move around on crutches for the next two years. Fortunately, she had been taken care of by a kind father-and-son team of doctors, who inspired her with their dedication and skill.

The untimely deaths of Robbie and her father, and Mary's ongoing illness confirmed for Jo the need for good doctors. "My native stubbornness made me decide to study medicine at all cost."

Her mother disliked the idea. It would cost a large portion of the family savings for Jo to go to medical school, and then what would come of it? Besides, Jenny didn't want her to live too far away.

One cold, early morning, Josephine and her mother had the same idea—a cup of hot cocoa—and they found themselves together in their big kitchen. They sat at the table and quietly sipped the cocoa, each afraid to speak first. Finally, her mother spoke: "If you really think you should, Jo, go ahead. I'll try not to fret too much about it." Josephine couldn't believe it. She was so thankful she jumped up and hugged her.

Few medical schools accepted women in the late 1890s. A friend suggested the Women's Medical College of the New York Infirmary. The college had been cofounded by Dr. Elizabeth Blackwell, the first woman in modern times to receive a medical degree, and her sister Dr. Emily Blackwell, who was the college's director.

The college's standards were high, and Josephine was required to study an entire year's worth of science courses in addition to many other courses before even being considered for admission. Jo worked vigorously and independently. At last, she passed the entrance examination and was ready to begin medical school.

Twenty-year-old Josephine was excited and a little sad. "I packed my bag and set out on my rather lonely great adventure. I knew that I had finally left my home and that I would never go back except for short visits."

Josephine was one of thirty-five women entering the Women's Medical College in 1894, and she was among the youngest. For the first few months, Jo was terribly homesick and afraid she had made an awful mistake in deciding to become a doctor.

Still, New York City in those days was an

enchanting place for a small-town girl like Josephine. Fifth Avenue was lined with brownstone townhouses. Horse-drawn carriages and buses clattered up and down the avenues. In the evening, the streets were lit by gaslight, which cast a warm, flickering glow.

Josephine lived in a respectable boardinghouse, along with other young women and men starting their careers. They became a kind of second family for each other, and they would pool their money to go to the theater.

Jo particularly liked attending vaudeville shows, the comedy song-and-dance performances. Sometimes Josephine would study as she watched, going over her "bag of bones." This was a set of human bones, which anatomy students used to memorize the parts of a skeleton. The thought of herself—a prim and proper young lady in a street-sweeping skirt and elaborately feathered hat—fingering away in the dark at the bones was almost as funny as the comedians on stage!

The other medical students all seemed more serious and studious to Josephine than herself. The course work was difficult for her at first, but eventually she excelled, ranking second in her graduating class. The only course she did not succeed in was called "The Normal Child," taught by Dr. Annie Sturges Daniel. It was the first class of its kind in any college. Dr. Daniel's theory was simple: Before a doctor can treat sick children, she must know what makes a normal child healthy.

After such amazing subjects as anatomy and chemistry, Josephine found the class boring. She didn't study, and she flunked it—her first and only failure in school. "It not only gave me a severe jolt to my pride," she wrote, "but roused in me a fierce anger at having to take the course over again the following year."

The next time she took the course, she listened carefully to Dr. Daniel's lectures and read every book she could find on the topic. To her surprise, she found it very intriguing. Ironically, it would turn out be the single most important training for her life's work.

Josephine graduated in 1898, one of only eighteen of the original thirty-five students in her class to finish. She had now earned the right to be called Dr. Baker. Because she was a woman, most hospitals would not even consider hiring her. She finally found a position as an intern at the New England Hospital for Women and Children in Boston, a hospital staffed entirely by women. Jo's friend and classmate, Dr. Florence Laighton, was also hired. As part of their duties, they had to spend three months working in the midst of the community.

Josephine and Florence were assigned to work at a clinic on Fayette Street in one of the poorest, most crowded sections of Boston. The clinic was surrounded by run-down tenements that housed recent immigrants. The people were squished, many to each room, with few places to wash and little to eat. Often more than one family lived in an apartment. Horrible smells of sewage, sweat, and rotting food drifted through the buildings and streets. Many people were sick from violent coughs, fevers, rashes, diarrhea, and drinking. Josephine was aghast at the misery.

Jo and Florence earned little more than their slum-dwelling patients. The young doctors lived together in the same boardinghouse, and each had four dollars a week to buy food. They survived on a diet of stew, baked beans, bread, and stewed prunes. On Sundays, they would treat themselves to a fancy meal at the Thorndike Hotel. This Sunday treat helped them face the depressing scenes of the week to come.

One day, Josephine was called to a filthy, one-room apartment to assist a woman who was about to have a baby. Cockroaches and bedbugs crawled everywhere. The pregnant woman, whose labor had already begun, was lying on a heap of straw in one corner. In another corner was her drunken husband.

As Josephine examined her patient, she found that the woman's back was one raw, festering sore. The patient whimpered that her husband had thrown a kettle of scalding water over her. Hearing the accusation, the man rushed at them in a rage.

Jo knew she had to act quickly to save herself, the woman, and the soon-to-be-born baby. She ran out into the hall, and he followed her. She had planned to run back inside the apartment and lock the door, but he was too quick and blocked her path. As he lurched toward her, Josephine clenched her fist and socked him. He was twice her weight, but the blow sent him reeling backward down the staircase.

The woman moaned, and Josephine hurried back into the room to finish delivering the baby. Afterward, she ran to the bottom of the stairs,

fearing she had accidentally killed the woman's husband. A neighbor came by and kicked him in the ribs, and the husband began to curse at them all. He was very much alive, and Jo was extremely relieved. "I think that in those relatively few moments I did more growing up than I had done in my previous twenty-odd years."

# 3

# Hell's Kitchen

At the end of their year as interns, Drs. Baker and Laighton planned to return to New York City. Josephine's mother and the rest of her family, however, argued that it would be much easier for Jo to start a practice in Poughkeepsie, where the Baker name was known and respected. They told her, "If you have enough money to support yourselves for five years entirely and for another five years in part, you stand a fighting chance in New York. If you haven't, New York is hopeless."

Josephine, of course, didn't have that much

money. Only a few hundred dollars remained of the money her mother had given her from the family savings. But Josephine and Florence refused to be discouraged from their goals. "Being young, we were incapable of worrying," Jo recalled.

So in 1900, the two doctors rented a four-story house on the west side of New York and put up their signs. They also indulged in buying an automobile—still a great luxury in those days. Then they waited for business to start pouring in.

As it turned out, business was little more than a trickle. A few pregnant women visited them and later returned with their children. But Dr. Baker's first-year earnings amounted to only $185. Even back then, that was hardly enough to pay the bills. Fortunately, Florence's family was more well off than Jo's, and they helped out with some expenses.

Still the young doctors refused to give up. Instead, they used ingenuity to create jobs for themselves. At the time, they were being pestered by a much-too-persistent life insurance salesman. When he mentioned they would have to have a medical examination to qualify for insurance coverage, Josephine asked matter-offactly for the name of the female medical examiner. The salesman was taken aback. He had never heard of such a thing—a female medical examiner!

The young women reminded him that they were doctors and showed him the door. But the thought lingered with them: Wouldn't women prefer to be examined by a female doctor?

The next day, they drove downtown, each to visit the office of one of the city's two biggest insurance companies, Equitable and New York Life. In both offices, the chief medical examiners laughed off their suggestions of becoming medical examiners. But when they stubbornly pointed out the advantages to female clients, both men relented and hired them as "special" medical examiners. Drs. Baker and Laighton became the first female medical examiners in the country to be employed by insurance companies.

The jobs provided both doctors with steady income. Among Josephine's clients was the world-famous singer and actress Lillian Russell. Jo was overwhelmed by Miss Russell's charm, beauty, and worldliness; and she spent the entire afternoon chatting with her. "It was one of my first red-letter days," Josephine remembered.

An opportunity to earn more money came along in 1901. One morning, Josephine noticed an item in the newspaper announcing that civil-service examinations would be held for the position of medical inspector for the city's Department of Health. The salary would be thirty dollars a month—double her first year's monthly income. Josephine took the examination and did well enough to be interviewed for a possible appointment by the health department's commissioner.

She arrived at the department headquarters, a dilapidated building that had once been the New York Athletic Club. She was shocked that the building was so old and dirty. She was even more shocked when she met the commissioner—a fat, blue-jowled, paunchy man who sat with his feet on his desk and chewed on a half-smoked cigar. Josephine expected to be grilled on medical knowledge. But he merely looked at her letter of recommendation—from a friend of her father who was also a political friend of the commissioner. With barely a word, he gave Dr. Baker the job. She was glad to have it, but it made her angry that it was her connections rather than her qualifications that got her the position.

If Jo's hiring had been a farce, so was her first assignment. Her job was to inspect three or four schools a day and in one hour determine which children were ill. If the children had diseases that were easily passed on, such as head lice, ringworm, or trachoma, they were to be sent home. But it was impossible to do the job well in so little time. Worse yet, some of the other inspectors never even bothered to go to their assigned schools. They were not fired, though, because the health department (and the city) was run by crooked politicians who gave jobs away to friends or to pay off favors.

Josephine worked hard at her job, but she was so disgusted by the situation that she planned to quit after her first year. However, in 1902, a new mayor was elected. Mayor Seth Low promptly got rid of all the loafers in the city offices. A new health commissioner and assistant sanitary superintendent were appointed. Dr. Walter Bensel, the assistant, convinced Josephine to stay in the department, and he offered her a new job at more than three times what she had been making.

Her new assignment was to hunt out and look after sick babies in the city slums. Among the worst of the slums was an area called Hell's Kitchen. This neighborhood was filled with newly arrived immigrants—Germans, Italians, Irish, and Russians, among others. With so many people squeezed into cramped and dirty quarters, diseases spread like wildfire. Each summer week, approximately 4,500 people died of cholera, dysentery, smallpox, meningitis, or other illnesses. A third of these victims were newborn babies.

Josephine's job was grueling. She worked from seven o'clock in the morning to six o'clock at night, climbing staircase after staircase, knocking on door after door in New York's poorest and most dangerous neighborhoods. The hot, humid summers and the long, tight dresses women were expected to wear made it that much more agonizing.

"It was the hardest physical labor I ever did in my life: just a backache and perspiration and disgust and discouragement and aching feet day in and day out," she recalled. One could hardly walk a block in any district without seeing a child's funeral procession. Yet, despite the seeming hopelessness of it all, she kept at the job. For the next five years, Dr. Baker roved the slums, doing what she could to improve the health of the babies she saw.

In 1907, she was given an unusual assignment—to track down a woman suspected of passing on typhoid fever. Mary Mallon, who eventually earned the nickname "Typhoid Mary," had been identified by the city health department as the cause of several outbreaks of the disease. Mary had once caught typhoid but recovered. Unfortunately, she then became a carrier of the disease, unwittingly spreading it to other people wherever she went. What was worse, she worked as a cook. Everyone who ate her food was exposed to the dreaded disease.

Josephine's task was to ask Mary to submit to a medical examination to check if she was in fact the suspected carrier. Other doctors had tried to examine the woman, but she had refused to cooperate or believe she could be a carrier. Mallon was now working as a cook in a prosperous home on Park Avenue, and Dr. Baker decided to pay her a surprise visit. Jo carefully positioned a policeman at the front of the house and one at the back to guard the escape routes. Then another policeman accompanied Jo as she entered the kitchen.

But Mary had been on the lookout. With a long fork in her hand, Mallon rushed toward Dr. Baker. Jo's quick reflexes saved her from being skewered, but in the confusion, Mary escaped into other rooms of the house. For the next three hours, Josephine and the policemen searched every nook and cranny of the house but could not find her.

Then a clue—a gap in the fence and footprints that led to the adjacent house. They searched that house but found no trace of the cook. Finally, just as they were about to give up, one of the policemen spotted a bit of blue calico material caught in a storage-room door beneath the front doorsteps. Pulling back the garbage cans in front of it, they opened the door. Out came Mallon swinging her fists. The policemen lifted her into the ambulance, and Dr. Baker sat on her all the way to the hospital. "It was like being in a cage with an angry lion," Josephine recalled.

Tests confirmed that Mallon was indeed a typhoid-fever carrier—the first ever documented in the United States. After Mary promised never again to work as a cook, she was released. Three years later, however, an outbreak of typhoid occurred at a New York hospital. Josephine decided to pay a visit. "Sure enough, there was Mary earning her living in the hospital kitchen and spreading typhoid germs among mothers and babies and doctors and nurses like a destroying angel," wrote Dr. Baker.

From that day on, to protect the public's health, Mary Mallon spent the rest of her life locked up. To her dying day, she remained convinced that she was not a typhoid carrier, even though the evidence was clear.

For the first time, Josephine realized the enormous power of public health authorities. Could that power be used to prevent diseases from happening rather than just to treat them?

In June 1907, Josephine was appointed to be the special assistant to the health commissioner. She began working with a research group looking for the causes of the city's scandalous death rate. Spurred by this project to look back on her visits with hundreds of poor families, Jo wondered if many deaths—especially those of babies and young children—could have been prevented if the mothers had been taught how to care for their children properly. "The way to keep people from dying from disease, it struck me suddenly, was to keep them from falling ill."

Because of the tragic findings of the research group, which supported Josephine's hunches, and her suggestion about prevention, the city created the Division of Child Hygiene in 1908. Dr. Baker was appointed its new chief. But before the new division could have money, the city leaders wanted evidence that prevention could lower the city's appalling death rate. Jo accepted the challenge.

That summer, together with a team of thirty school nurses, Josephine visited the homes of newborns in a slum district on the Lower East Side. Hours after a baby had been brought home from the hospital, Josephine or one of her nurses would check on the mother. They would give her advice on keeping the baby healthy—bathe the baby frequently; give the newborn lots of fresh air and sunlight; breast-feed the child; dress the baby in thin clothing in the summer's heat. Most of these suggestions are common sense by today's standards, but then much of it was new to both health workers and the public.

By the end of the summer, it was time to find out whether or not Dr. Baker's experiment had been a success. She was confident, but even she was surprised at the results. In the one district where Dr. Baker and her team had worked, the death rate had been cut by 1,200 people. Everywhere else in town, the death rate had been as bad as ever.

Beyond her wildest hopes, Dr. Baker had proven the worth of preventive public health care. The city leaders were so pleased they gave her a generous budget to begin working on a citywide disease prevention program. The division was the first governmentally funded agency devoted exclusively to children's health. Jo noted, "That was the actual beginning of my life's work."

# The Fight for Children's Health

Thirty-five-year-old Josephine knew the Division of Child Hygiene faced many problems. But she took some comfort in the fact that her new staff would consist of trained professionals—doctors like herself with whom she had worked for many years. Was Dr. Baker ever in for a surprise!

No sooner had her male colleagues received notices of their appointments to her new division when all six of them marched into her office and handed her their resignations. "It was nothing personal, they assured me, but they could not reconcile taking orders from a woman," she recalled.

"See here," she told the men, "you are really crying before you are hurt. I quite realize that you may not like the idea of working for me as a woman. But isn't there another side of this question? I do not know whether I am going to like working with you."

Josephine proposed a deal with the doctors: Work on my staff for one month. If at the end of that period you still want to leave, I will not stand in your way.

Reluctantly, the men agreed.

One month later, when Josephine reminded them it was time to make a decision, they told her they had no intention of quitting. Their jobs were far too challenging to give up. All six stayed for many years.

Besides facing prejudice against women, Josephine also had her hands full with trying to outmaneuver corrupt politicians. Shortly after the Division of Child Hygiene was created, a powerful group of politicians started giving public health jobs to their friends rather than to the people who were most qualified. On many occasions, Jo risked losing her job by refusing to let unqualified appointees into her department. Eventually, the politicians came to respect her toughness and integrity.

Having won the confidence of her staff and city leaders, Jo was free to put her time and energy into saving children's lives. But where to begin? There were no child-health programs anywhere in the world to serve as a guide. She had already expanded the experimental program of educating new mothers into a citywide effort. But that did not help the hundreds of babies who were dying during childbirth.

Josephine figured that much of the problem was due to ignorance on the part of the "midwives." Midwives are women who assist mothers in childbirth. In Europe at this time, where most of the immigrants came from, midwives were more popular than doctors. This tradition continued after the immigrants arrived in New York. And even if these mothers wanted their babies born in a hospital with a doctor's help, most could not afford it.

Jo had a good deal of respect for midwives.

She once said that if she ever had a daughter who was pregnant, she would prefer the childbirth be assisted by a qualified midwife rather than a doctor. But most midwives in New York City had no official training. As a result, babies often died or were injured unnecessarily.

Hundreds of babies who survived were accidentally blinded at birth. Hospital-born babies were given a drop of silver-nitrate solution in each eye to prevent an infectious disease often caught during birth. But many midwives didn't know about the eye solution.

The first step Josephine took was to register midwives and develop a training program for them. After they completed the required course work, they were each issued a license to serve as a midwife. Eventually, Dr. Baker helped found a school to train midwives at Bellevue Hospital Medical School.

With training programs in place, Josephine knew that midwives understood how and when to give newborns eyedrops. Unfortunately, though, the midwives often used a solution that had become contaminated or had evaporated to a dangerously high concentration. The midwives had no way of testing the solution before using it.

Josephine tackled this problem by inventing a new way to package the solution. Rather than bottles, she had the liquid sealed in beeswax capsules, with just enough for each eye. Within a few years, most of the city's cases of baby blindness had disappeared.

That wasn't the last time Jo called upon her inventive wit. She discovered that some babies were being accidentally suffocated by their tight, binding clothing. So she developed a sewing pattern for baby clothes that opened down the front. The clothes became so popular that the McCall's Pattern Company bought the design. Josephine earned a penny royalty fee on every pattern sold. The Metropolitan Life Insurance Company ordered 200,000 copies of the pattern to be distributed to its policyholders.

In addition to immigrant children, Jo was concerned about orphaned babies. At a hospital that cared for abandoned babies, over half the babies died, and no one knew why. The staff of nurses and doctors was among the best in the city. Josephine inspected the facility and found it spotless. So why were the babies dying?

On a hunch, she took some of the babies from the hospital and put them into the care of trained mothers in the tenements. The death rate was cut in half.

Josephine concluded that the babies at the orphan hospital were missing the cuddling and love they needed. Rarely handled by nurses, the babies were dying of loneliness. The same thing was happening to many babies born to the city's wealthy families whose children were cared for by professional nurses.

Dr. Baker was one of the first doctors to recognize how important being held is to a child's health. She began the first organized foster-mother program. Women were paid to care for orphaned babies in their homes as if they were the babies' real mothers.

Another of Jo's early achievements at the Division of Child Hygiene was the creation of baby health stations. Most milk bought by poor people was unpasteurized, so the milk spoiled easily. Bad milk was one of the leading sources of early childhood diseases. To address this problem, New York City had a few milk stations, which provided poor people with fresh pasteurized milk at a low price. But Josephine wanted to increase the number of stations, and she had another idea as well. When the mothers come for milk, why not give them some free advice on parenting?

The baby health stations would cost money, however, and the city was not willing to fund them. So Jo went directly to Mrs. J. Borden Harriman, a wealthy woman interested in children's health. Mrs. Harriman formed a fund-raising committee that gathered enough money to support thirty new baby health stations. Eventually, these baby stations cared for more than 60,000 underprivileged babies.

Not long after starting up the baby health stations, Josephine read a book by John Spargo called *The Bitter Cry of the Children*. It made her aware of the babies who weren't getting proper care because they were left in the care of older sisters when their parents went to work. The book called these girls "little mothers." Despite their best efforts, these little mothers knew very little about proper parenting. The babies in their care often became ill or even died.

Jo remembered how much she had liked to join clubs when she was a girl. So she began the Little Mother's League, a club to teach young girls about basic baby care. The young girls of the Little Mother's League were not only good students, but they became Dr. Baker's helpers.

"These youngsters were our most efficient missionaries," said Josephine, "canvassing tenements for us, cajoling mothers...into giving the baby health stations a trial, checking up on mothers who backslid in attendance at the stations, telling every mother they met all about what they were learning." The girls also organized "fresh-air outings" for their mothers and baby brothers and sisters. They even wrote and performed plays about how to take care of babies and toddlers properly.

When the newspapers began reporting on the success of the Little Mother's League, letters started pouring in from India, China, Japan, Turkey, and countries in Europe. These people wanted advice on how to start their own programs, and Dr. Baker gave it.

She had realized that many of the programs she was creating could be used in other cities. In 1909, she had cofounded an organization that could help spread the word about preventive health care for children around the nation. It became known as the American Child Hygiene Association.

A few years later, Jo made a deal with herself: She would retire when every state in the Union had organized a bureau just like New York City's. As part of the plan, she helped establish the national Children's Bureau in 1912. She served as its adviser for the next sixteen years.

By the end of 1913, Josephine was forty years old and managing the health of the 1.2 million schoolchildren who lived in New York City. She also continued to hold down a private practice. Almost certainly, much of the money she was earning was being sent home to her mother and sister, who still lived in the family home in Poughkeepsie. The family's investment in Jo's education had paid off well.

In the early part of 1914, the city government once again changed hands. The "Reformers" took office. They were determined to rid the government of any dishonesty in politics. All full-time city employees were forced by the Reformers to give up their outside work to prove their dedication to their jobs. Dr. Baker had to choose between her private practice and her job as head of the Division of Child Hygiene. Though Dr. Baker probably could have earned more money in her private practice, she chose the health department.

Josephine also had to take a series of civil-service

examinations, given to all government employees to measure their abilities. If she failed to do well, she could lose her job.

It was a very hot summer day when she came to take the exam. It was the most difficult test Jo had ever encountered. The written part lasted the entire day. And the oral test was conducted by a board of New York's best children's doctors.

After it was over, Josephine had to wait a few months to find out how she had done. Not only did she have to pass all sections of the test to keep her position, but she also had to do better than all of the competitors.

The test results finally arrived—she passed with a grade of 94. Her nearest competitor had scored an 86.

# Right to Vote, Right to Health

In her mid forties, Josephine's life revolved around two beliefs she held strongly: everyone—including children—should have the right to good health; and women should have rights equal to those of men. In 1908, Jo had worked with five women to start the College Women's Equal Suffrage League. Since females were banned by law from voting, the organization argued for their right to do so. Over the years, Jo had grown more and more outspoken about her convictions.

She frequently wrote letters to newspapers and spoke on street corners. She would stop her car at a curb on Wall Street, Columbus Circle, or Union Square, then stand up and begin talking about the importance of women's right to vote.

Inevitably, an audience would soon gather, almost always male. And they weren't shy about heckling her: "Why aren't you home where you belong?" "Women don't want to vote—it's just the old maids." "Who's going to mind the baby when you're out voting?" At first, Josephine was afraid to keep speaking, but after a while she learned to talk back. She grew more confident, using humor to disarm the crowd.

Each year, Jo would march down Fifth Avenue in the annual suffragist parade. It was first held in 1908, when she was one of only five hundred who marched. Seven years later, it had turned into one of the most impressive parades in America. Thousands of women from various walks of life participated. Josephine strode down the street among the college women, who wore caps and gowns. There were all-female bands and a cavalry of women on horseback. Hundreds of men who believed in women's right to vote also marched.

By 1915, Dr. Baker was New York City's leading expert on children's health. That year, Dr. William H. Park, dean of the New York University Medical School, asked her to lecture to his students on child hygiene. Her lecture was to be given as part of a new degree in public health. At the time, women were not allowed to enroll in the school, so Josephine offered the dean a bargain: I will lecture on child hygiene if you allow me to enroll in the degree program.

Dr. Park was miffed, and he absolutely refused her offer. He was not having a woman tell him how to run his school. He would find someone else. But *there was no one else*. After all, Josephine had almost single-handedly created the concept of child hygiene programs for the public. He returned again to Dr. Baker, and again she refused unless he met her one condition. Finally, the dean surrendered. Having changed the rules for Josephine, the school now had to allow other women to enroll.

Thinking she had won the battle, Josephine showed up at the school to deliver her first lecture. As soon as she began to talk, all the students— still men at the time—began to clap very loudly. The students were upset that a woman was teaching them a class. Jo was scared, but that didn't stop her.

"I threw back my head and roared with laughter, laughing at them and with them at the same time—and they stopped, as if somebody turned a switch," she said later.

The students remained silent as she presented her lecture. However, the moment she ended her presentation, the unruly clapping began again. Jo lectured at the medical school once annually for fifteen years, from 1915 to 1930. And every time, she was clapped in and out in the same rude manner.

During the early years of her teaching, war was being waged between the nations of Europe. In 1917, the United States became involved.

The Division of Child Hygiene had had plenty of publicity before the war. But government officials around the world suddenly realized that if they were going to have boys to fight the wars of the future, they would have to take care of them now. Foreign dignitaries flocked to New York to see how Dr. Baker's Division of Child Hygiene worked. Officials from other American cities also began paying her visits.

Josephine wrote that it took "the sinister stimulus of mass murder to make the fighting nations see the necessity for saving children."

Dr. Baker's expertise was so much in demand that a large international charity organization asked her to give up her post in New York City and take charge of all the refugees flooding into France. She had already accepted the position when a telegram arrived a day later from the highest levels of government in Washington, D.C. It said: "Dr. Baker, you are needed more at home than abroad; please tell them you have changed your mind."

Josephine reluctantly agreed. Shortly afterward, she was appointed assistant surgeon general in the United States government with the rank of major. Dr. Baker was the first woman ever to receive such a high-ranking government position.

One curious result of the war was that many Americans came to believe that only European children were suffering. In reality, American children were suffering too. Donations that used to be given to poor American families were now going overseas. To make matters worse, the war caused food prices to rise sharply. Many people could no longer afford to eat properly.

Shortly after the United States entered the war, Josephine was walking down Fifth Avenue. The street was strewn with American flags and filled with soldiers on the way to Europe to fight. She met a woman in a bright new khaki uniform who was soon setting sail for London.

She was going to supervise the feeding of school-children there. Wasn't it horrible, the woman asked, that on account of the war twelve percent of them were undernourished?

"That is horrible," Jo replied, "but what would you say if I told you that in New York twenty-one percent of the schoolchildren are undernourished, and largely on account of the same war."

This was a serious problem, but the public's attention was focused on Europe. So Dr. Baker made the following statement to the *New York Times:* "It's six times safer to be a soldier in the trenches of France than to be born a baby in the United States."

Some people said her statement was unpatriotic. But it was true: American soldiers were dying at the rate of four percent; infants in the United States were dying at a rate of twelve percent. Her statement made Americans aware of the plight of their hungry children.

Because of this new awareness, Jo was able to start a citywide school lunch program, which became a model for the world. As a result of the program, the percentage of undernourished children in New York dropped almost as low as it was in London by the end of the war in 1918.

While the war was still in progress, the women's right-to-vote movement made a concerted effort to enlist the aid of President Woodrow Wilson. One evening, Josephine received a call from Mrs. Norman Whitehouse, the leader of the New York State suffragists. Mrs. Whitehouse told her that the president had consented to receive a small group of women for suffrage, and Dr. Baker was invited.

The group was nervous as it waited in a room outside the White House's Oval Office. Would the president support their movement?

President Wilson appeared and shook hands with each of them. Then he made a speech to them that was better than they had even hoped for. The president gave his wholehearted support for women's right to vote. "As we went back to New York, we all felt that our fight had finally been won there in the White House reception room," Josephine remembered.

They were right. Shortly thereafter, the Nineteenth Amendment was passed on August 18, 1920, giving women the right to vote.

# ⑥
# Winning the Fight

In 1918, New York City elected a new mayor, John F. "Red Mike" Hylan. After taking office, he did everything in his power to have Dr. Baker fired—for no apparent reason. After he failed, she found out he thought she was someone else!

While Red Mike was working to get her fired, Cyrus McCormick, a wealthy Chicago industrialist, was trying to hire her. He had founded a child health institution in his hometown, and he wanted Dr. Baker to run it. Money was no object. She could name her salary. But she said no. For better or worse, Josephine loved her city and her job. "I had fought my way through so many battles, private and public, in New York . . . that to consider leaving it was like considering an operation that would completely change my personality."

Soon after McCormick's offer, Jo was offered the position of health director for the whole London school system. Again, she said no.

Josephine's work as a champion for children's health rights occasionally merged with her fight for women's rights. In 1921, she accepted an invitation to explain to the United States Congress why she supported a bill to provide maternity benefits to working mothers. The bill failed to pass, but she kept up the fight for women's and children's rights through many articles, including a regular column in the *Ladies Home Journal.*

Five books by Dr. Baker were published from 1921 to 1925: *Healthy Babies, Healthy Mothers, Healthy Children, The Growing Child,* and *Child Hygiene.* These titles established Dr. Baker as the world's foremost expert in child hygiene. Over the next decade, Jo authored more than sixty-six articles for professional publications and over one hundred articles for popular magazines and newspapers. It was during this period that she began signing her name "S. Josephine Baker," so as not to be confused with the famous jazz dancer Josephine Baker.

Jo had fulfilled her goal of establishing a child hygiene department in every state by 1923, so she officially retired. The record she left spoke for itself. Before the Division of Child Hygiene was established, the city's infant death rate had been 144 deaths for every 1,000 births. By 1923, it had dropped to 66 deaths, the lowest rate among the world's major cities. Her leadership had resulted in saving more than 82,000 lives.

Josephine's retirement from the Division of Child Hygiene did not mark the end of her career. From 1922 to 1924, she represented the United States on the Health Committee of the League of Nations, the forerunner of the United Nations. Dr. Baker was the first woman to be a professional representative to the league. During her "retirement," she also worked as a member of over twenty-five medical societies, served as a consultant to the New York State Department of Health, and continued to lecture to graduate students in public health at New York University, as well as at Columbia University.

Josephine's mother, Jenny, died in 1924, and

her sister, Mary, in 1927. These deaths left her with deep sadness, but with fewer family responsibilities. Now free to travel, Jo lectured on children's health throughout the United States and journeyed overseas. She went to Russia in 1934 with her friend, the novelist Ida (I.A.R.) Wylie. Upon her return, Josephine wrote about visiting the world's "most outstanding example of a widespread, comprehensive system of child welfare."

In 1935, at sixty-two, Dr. S. Josephine Baker took office as the president of the American Medical Women's Association. Her final years were spent at a farm outside of Princeton, New Jersey. The farm was called Trevenna, which is Cornish for "house belonging to women." Jo lived there with Ida Wylie, Elizabeth Embler, a former New York City schoolteacher, and Dr. Louise Pearce, the scientist who discovered the cure for sleeping sickness. In this peaceful setting, she wrote her life story, *Fighting for Life*.

In 1945, at the age of seventy-one, Josephine died of cancer in New York Hospital. People throughout New York City, the nation, and the world felt sadness at her passing, recognizing the good she had accomplished.

Dr. S. Josephine Baker was once asked whether her pioneering work for children's health had been worth it. "Oh, yes," Jo said. "I can still see the light in a mother's eye when her baby was assured of health."

# Bibliography

**Books and Interviews**

Baker, S. Josephine, M.D. *Fighting for Life*. New York: Robert E. Krieger, 1980 (reprint of 1939 edition).

Bellemeade (New Jersey) Historical Society. Personal interview with local historian Ursula Brecknell, 1992.

Dutchess County Historical Society. Correspondence, 1991-92.

Imperato, Pascal James, M.D. *The Administration of a Public Health Agency*. New York: Human Sciences Press, 1983.

Rosen, George, M.D., and Beate Caspari-Rosen, M.D. *400 Years of a Doctor's Life*. New York: Henry Schuman, 1947.

Spargo, John. *The Bitter Cry of Children*. New York: MacMillan, 1906.

Vale, Ethlie Ann, and Greg Ptacek. *Mothers of Invention*. New York; William Morrow, 1988.

Wylie, Ida Alexa Rose. *My Life with George, An Unconventional Autobiography*. New York: Random House, 1940.

**Articles**
(including obituaries)

*Medical Women's Journal.* May 1945.

*New York Times.* May 17, 1918; January 17, 1943; February 23, 1945.

*Poughkeepsie Daily Eagle.* May 28, 1890.

*Poughkeepsie New Yorker.* February 22, 1945.

*Poughkeepsie Sunday Courier.* June 1, 1890.

*The Princetonian.* March 19, 1959.